GW01159163

Your Light

Wendy McInnes and Wendo's Light

Published by Wendo's Light, 2024.

YOUR LIGHT

First edition. October 21, 2024.

ISBN: 979-8227305428

Written by Wendy McInnes and Wendo's Light.

Table of Contents

I dedicate this book to my husband Steven, my kid, the biggest mirrors and catalysts.

To the collective may the vibration continue to rise.

To source thank you for my existence.

Introduction

This is my writing. Please be respectful of copywriting. This book is written with love and the intention of sharing knowledge for free.

I want to put a special thank you to all who helped with the editing of this book, as well as my Husband, Child and close friends for your support all these years.

My gratitude to Fiona and Medium Omar MJ for their editing. The written word is not my strength. The people we surround ourselves with make a huge impact. I would not be where I am without them.

Welcome with love. In this book, I share the resources, methods, and current opinions I have gained on my Journey. The general spiritual philosophy I follow is that we are all one. A part or fragment of God/Creator/Source etc. We are powerful, beautiful beings. It has colored my personal and spiritual growth. I have experienced this as an empowering way to welcome increased energetic awareness and consciousness. I feel sharing this right away is important because, regarding working with energy and spirit, I acknowledge that negative beings/energies exist and have things we can learn from them. They are not to be feared as we can stand in a place of love and claim sovereignty. The only power they could have is what we grant them consciously or subconsciously. Our interactions can be catalysts for our growth just as with other in-body beings. So just a heads up that in later areas this is the perspective taken. I realize not everyone agrees, so if your beliefs differ greatly this may not be something that resonates with you. I do not work or collaborate with beings not of love in general but have interacted with them, this goes along the lines of attachments, rescue and transition/stuck spirits/soul retrieval, and the like.

I do mainly inner child/reparenting style mental/emotional healing and touch on that. The exercises focus on gaining a deeper understanding through direct experience of what we are, i.e. a being of energy. It is a good foundation for psychic/mediumship development.

1

I believe that the healing process can be as easy or as hard as our current programming (subconscious, beliefs etc.) makes it. For example, a part of ourselves believes we deserve pain and so our healing process is more painful. Or maybe, we are very curious about why. Why we came to this incarnation also needs to be taken into account, maybe you want to heal quickly but something about the lessons causes it to go slowly. Therefore, a level of awareness of the process or self may be needed. I encourage you to ask spirit and your higher self for help on all stages of the journey. Spirit and other energies have been some of the biggest support and catalysts in my growth. This book may be updated as I move along on my journey and the resources etc. grow.

A note on the importance of inner work with psychic development. The physical body stores traumas and is also the root of the energy antenna for psychic information. If we use a window analogy, then the more trauma there is, the more dirt on the window you are trying to see through. The lower frequencies are stuck there. There are many ways you can approach this but I believe a holistic well-rounded approach is helpful. Working with the energy of the body, mind, emotions, and energy centers. Healing in one area will ripple to start healing other areas Mental/emotional/physical/spiritual, they are all connected. There may come a point when you become just the soul and you do not identify with your past. You become the self that is now. This is a loose road map for holistic self-actualization.

Disclaimer

I am not a professional therapist or counselor. This is for entertainment purposes only etc. I have not taken many, if any, courses on psychology or any of these methods. I speak 100% from my own learning and experience. I claim no responsibility for the results or what you do with this knowledge, besides how this book can help people. I wrote this book so I would not be repeating myself when starting to work with someone or in practice circles which may focus on some of the exercises mentioned in the energy chapter. This is the basic knowledge I feel all could benefit from. I hope to save time and keep practice circles focused. (the personal growth of writing the book was awesome) The psychologically related things are just because it's all important, but that's just my opinion. I feel this basic knowledge will deepen results when someone books with me. Basic Mental health should be in the school curriculum.

Chakras

Chakras are energy centers within our bodies, according to ancient Indian spiritual traditions like Hinduism and Buddhism. There are seven main chakras that run along the spine, each associated with specific organs, emotions, and aspects of our lives. They are often perceived to be swirling wheels of energy that regulate various bodily functions and emotions. There is plenty of information available about them. There are many above and below your body as well as in all your joints. The Chinese meridians are interesting especially if you want to heal your physical body. In this book, some of the exercises will assist you in feeling these in your body. When doing the mental and emotional work you may feel sensations or notice some kind of change in these chakras over time.

Mediumship

Mediumship refers to the ability of a person, known as a medium, to communicate with spirits or entities from the spirit world. Mediums act as intermediaries between the physical world and the spirit realm, conveying messages, information, or guidance from deceased individuals or spiritual beings to those seeking communication or closure. Mediumship practices vary widely across cultures and belief systems, often involving techniques such as channeling, trance states, or psychic abilities to facilitate communication with spirits. This type of experience often happens naturally and someone referring to themselves as a medium often practices to develop their abilities. I believe it is important to know how and where your information is coming from. A medium is always a psychic, however not all psychics are trained mediums. If you would like to develop this in a deeper way, I mention in the references places I found helpful and often free below. This is just a small intro to the topic, as it is covered more in depth below.

Mental And Emotional Healing

This chapter will cover psychological/emotional methods of healing, such as methods to help with neuroplasticity/brain rewiring and releasing emotions and stored energies, thus creating a relationship with yourself. Doing this work can ripple and assist the healing of the body. This transforms dark to light, Self Hate To Deeper Self Love and Appreciation. It increases our capacity for self-kindness and compassion. Inner harmony corresponds to less resistance. It seems hard, but is worth it. I am not one to have to fight to change a habit. I do this to tip the balance in energy, more for creating the new me, less attached to the old me. Later I share how/why I started doing these methods. You are worth investing in yourself.

At the start, we can often need someone to help or hold space for us as we do this work. I encourage everyone to seek help, especially at the beginning. You are worth the investment of time and money.

Self-inquiry is powerful. Why do I do this? Why is this habit so hard to change? The methods below are ways to get the answers when working on our own.

Our goal is to get through the layers of the onion to the center, the pure soul/truth of what we are. Thought is so powerful and it affects our physical body and nervous system. It may be needed to work in the way mentioned or similar to de-program, remove energy, and heal the nervous system so we can live a more soulful/authentic etc. life; at least that has been my experience.

When I refer to parts I am talking about an aspect of ourselves that is often an inner child that is stuck in time due to trauma and maybe subconsciously influencing us, often seen as a habit, belief, or could be a trigger of any kind. Maybe referred to Sub-personalities or fragments in other psychology methods. Internal Family Systems uses the term parts but I do not think I refer to it in the same way.

The book I love "Healing The Fragmented Selves Of Trauma Survivors" by Janina Fisher has some great information on how to work with parts. I suggest reading it. Having help working with many can be good, as it can be a challenge to ask questions of the parts while also being in their experiences/feelings.

The key when doing this healing is looking at all aspects of ourselves and loving them/providing a need. Due to many types of trauma or environments, the parts often had or have an important job. They kept us safe or were rejected because of survival. You are alive and here now; keeping this in mind will help.

Things to always do when working with parts

● If the part is a past part in time, ask if they would like to come forward

● After feeling and hearing what they have to say, ask what they need to feel, and how you want them to feel about the topic. Maybe you need to take action in life or build them a place to visit till they are ready to integrate.

● They are always allowed to have the feelings they do. You are also allowed to feel how you feel about them. All feelings are valid. It can feel a little back and forth when feeling you now and the part of yourself from the past/subconscious.

I think the most important thing to stress here, besides being curious, compassionate, etc, is YOU have the ideas and constructs that will work best for YOU, bringing subconscious things to consciousness. If you are working with someone and they are guiding you through an experience (meditation, exercise) but a different thing comes up, say instead of a hot spring, you come to a luke warm stream that is okay. Just go with what comes to you. We have the answers inside ourselves.

Timeline Healing (may have other names) is the concept that the past is just energy. With respect to neuroplasticity, it is proven that memories can be altered permanently. I refer here to not sticking to one memory but setting the intention for all that emotion/similar memory energy to be transformed like a line where you put events on it. It is just energy and you can shift from a young age to the present time by traveling along it. All the energy between point A and the present can be transformed. Intent is very powerful because you are powerful.

Discernment is also not a bad thing, though some of our inner parts can appear ugly and scary. If you are energetically sensitive or can see things, it may seem it is not yours. It can sometimes be challenging to tell, however as you go and learn your energy, you can feel the energy difference. Though sometimes those can have energetic resonance with our affairs. So, try to use discernment and get to know yourself. One helpful thing here is when you are looking at the thing: are you looking within or without? Find the thing that the outside thing is having resonance with, heal it and that thing has no reason to be around. This will be discussed more in the energy sections.

Inner Child and Shadow can often get confused. Very BASICALLY, the shadow is often ATTRIBUTES of personality rejected, whereas the inner child tends to be a wounded child fragment. Both affect your actions, thoughts, and beliefs subconsciously.

The basics of inner/wounded child healing, in my experience, is based on providing for the child things which you did not receive. The first thing here is to hear the inner child and its feelings. What is the wound? You will need a perfect mother and father mental construct/ archetype to parent that child and if you are not able to feel what it would feel like to have that need met, this may be difficult. I have not studied Internal family systems though I have been told that this is similar to that. Many of these methods are used in various therapies. You can attempt to re-make the memory. Anything you can think of to use, just apply it as needed. Feel towards the child to the best of your ability what you want to heal. Sometimes you will need to go slowly, other times flying/traveling the timeline is enough.

The key here is that the child is you, how would you feel about this child if it was yours? This allows you to give to yourself that which you did not have or whatever wound you are working with.

Using the timeline analogy will help transmute the energy through time as well. It is how to apply inner parenting for a particular topic through time. You can have all of the inner children along the timeline jump on/in that need that healing on that topic. With this timeline work, you are changing the energetics of your past. Changing the memories or at least the way they impact you.

This topic is always good for anyone at any stage and as an example. You deserve to be celebrated and loved just because you exist. The idea is that you have even more love in this current moment because you transmuted the energy in the timeline.

First step. Start where you are i.e. pregnant, just conceived, this life inside of you. It has not even done anything, it just came into existence. Marvel at it. Picture it as it is growing in you. (if you are a man/male you can imagine your "perfect partner/mother' of a child and how you would support)

In each stage going forward:

Feel the amazingness of its existence. Feel the excitement, encouragement, belief in its goodness, and deserving of love.

Next, give birth to it. Look at it, go through and imagine doing some basic caring for it (feeding, diapering). Pour all the feelings you can muster about how special, lovable, etc. that it is into the child. It's so innocent and pure.

1. Get onto some power animal (giant bird, lion, horse, etc.) or vehicle and travel up the whole of your timeline into the current moment. Imagine all through the timeline all this feeling saturating yourself with this energy. Picture the line of time. So it is as if you have had this love just because you exist all through the time. Imagine it rippling out and healing anything it can.

2. Wrap the timeline up like a ball of string. Imagine it as a color. Put it in water, and move it around. To dry it unwrap the ball

and with a hand smooth/dry it with the new feeling/frequency you want.

3. You can stop at ages if your mind brings you to an age. That you have a mother and father who are perfect and love you just because you exist in this. You are also the parent here. How would you want to be to your child in the moment you are remaking? How would it be different? Make it that way. Stop as many times as you need to. It doesn't have to be perfect. Just do your best. Bring the feeling to your current self.

If you are working with a particular part(s) here, make sure to ask them if they want to be brought forward in time. If they are ready to be reabsorbed into the now or if they need more time. If ready, imagine a method that feels right to you for them to do so.

I often imagine hugging and then absorbing them. Or dancing with my perfect mother, father, the child, and me around a fire. As we dance they slide into me until I am alone around the fire. These both result in increased power and self-love. You are after all bringing all that work into you now.

This is just a basic outline and concept. I would love to hear how you adapted this or if it inspired you in your healing.

Meeting an aspect of self: Inner Child or Shadow

I use a few methods here. Feel free to change. You have all the best answers for yourself inside of you. I also added some that have come up with people I have worked with. Traveling down tends to signify the subconscious. (In mediumship or to meet guides Journey up)

1. The Forest Clearing

In your imagination go to a clearing. Ask any aspect of the self that is the cause of a habit or what you are working on to come out. Then watch the forest. Depending on how it wishes to be perceived it will come out. Maybe an animal or a wild-looking person/child. Sometimes it may be afraid. Give it time, and follow what you feel to gain its trust. Maybe food or clothing. Defiantly feeling of curiosity and acceptance of whatever that part shows itself as. (Be discerning and curious, trust your gut, not everything is you aka attachments).

1. The Hallway

Open a door to a hallway with many doors. Open a door. What is inside? How does the part(s) inside react to you? What does the room look like? (the first part I ever found was with this method. I swore the room was one I had, though my mother always said I never had a room like that).

1. The Cave

Go down into a cave, maybe a door, or you dig something out from the cave.

1. The Well

Going to the bottom of a well type of space either with stairs or some other way. Be sure to bring it out.

Depending on what state your part is in it may need to be brought out bathed and cared for. Usually, I take mine to a special place I have already set up for resting myself. Though sometimes a place will just appear. You will know the right thing to do at the moment.

Building Something Together

This is a method for intent going from old to new. This is helpful for working to change beliefs. You can use the transmuted energy or anger to build something new. A broken down wall, into a path or foundation to a house, adding intent for the new feelings and beliefs.

In the self-worth dragon story(See Table Of Contents), I continued to work with other parts and aspects/energies in me to build the rest of the house. When everything was ready and integrated I was not able to access the house anymore because it all became a permanent part of my psyche. The thing to remember is you always have the answers. There is no right or wrong way. Build a castle, tree house, or underground bunker if that is what is needed at the time. It can always change and grow with you.

Working With Multiple Parts

Sometimes we have more than one part to work with. I have found that making them all different rooms or spaces helpful. Then you can go to the place they are and visit.

My first Multi Parts Experience

The very first place I had was a clearing and off the clearing were paths. At the end of each path was a space for the part. My first group of parts was the rebel, Pin-up girl/sexual, wild woman, spiritual nun type. After a couple of months of working with these, I gained an understanding of them and how they need to be expressed or were influencing me. To finish, we all danced around a glowing white fire, eventually, we wound around each other creating a big tree trunk pillar of light. We became one and healed. After this experience, all visits were just with the tree, a feeling of love and acceptance.

When working with conflicting parts, feel how each feels about the topic/issue. Then notice/feel how they feel about each other. Is there a way they can compromise, or help each other? It can be helpful to journal and label the parts and then go between them. Having help working with many can be good, as it can be a challenge to ask questions of the parts while also being in their experiences/feelings.

Example

One is scared or weak feeling about something and the other is aggressive and protective in that area. At first, the protective one may feel angry or disdainful towards the weaker one. After, they see the reason that the scared one is the way it is and that maybe it has been protecting it all this time but they have not been aware of each other. The Protective part can help the scared part feel safe then because the scared part feels safe the protective part can relax and be less alert. Thus creating inner harmony and less fear/anger. Gaining awareness of these inner conflicts and resolving them brings peace.

Shamanic Methods

This is a meditative practice where the shaman enters an altered state of consciousness to travel to the spiritual realms, often referred to as the Upper World, Middle World, and Lower World. I have not used the Middle World. I just use this basic construct not one to do many big rituals or tools though I see the benefit of doing so. These are basic constructs for you to build on.

You can go up or down. The lower realm/world is more the realm of the internal self. Up is towards spirit. Maybe one of the reasons why in mediumship circle meditations we go up, at least in the ones I have attended and facilitated. Think of it like going up the chakras like a ladder. The root is survival/basic body needs, crown higher spiritual self-access.

One of my favorite Multi-application is the Hot Spring of Forgiveness

1. Walk through a forest till you come to a big tree. Walk around till you find an opening in the roots.

2. Go through the hole and down.

3. Come out at a crystal cave with a hot spring. There may be a spirit guide there to take your things.

4. The aspect of yourself from some time that needs forgiveness is waiting in there. The water is always gently flowing so it always cleans.

5. There is a special bar of soap you pick up and wash the part/aspect with.

6. Get all the parts, toes, fingers & everywhere.

7. When you are done, hug this part and have them melt into you clean and forgiven. Then go back out.

8. Maybe the guide would give you something if one was there.

Feel free to use this for other things or just a place to be loving to yourself.

On my YouTube Channel Wendo's_Light, there is an explanation of doing a similar thing but with fire, and after that you come to this pool to finish the meditation.

These are all ways to work with the psyche. It seems these days we are so much in the mind and not often in our body. Thoughts are what set the frequency/vibration of energy. Very powerful. The inner work can help us understand and shift our thinking and behavior. However, I would like to point out it's all energy. The space between matter and what effects matter.

Story Of The Self-Worth Dragon

Special Thank you to Megan Britton for editing this story so it reads beautifully.

Once there was a dragon whose responsibility was to hold the beliefs of Sally's self-worth. The dragon was a thought form, which is just the result of the energy of belief reinforced over time. Sally had not realized she had created the dragon, because she was young and unaware of how powerful these thoughts are. One day, Sally realized her old beliefs around her self worth had changed. Through time and growth her beliefs had changed, so she wanted to replace her old beliefs about herself with new ones that aligned to her newer self. However, even though she did not agree with the old beliefs, they were still there.

This dragon was created from repetitive thoughts of low self worth and wasn't ready to go away. It was fed from years of the same thoughts, behaviors, and even outside sources that only reinforced it's power. This dragon became very strong within the creator. So strong that it knew how to blend in and hide it's influence and subconscious expression on Sally. The younger, scared, hurt, shamed parts of Sally fed into the dragon enough so that it became a force of sharp teeth and claws with excellent grip. The dragon also saw itself as the protector of the version of Sally that created the dragon in the first place.

Even though Sally was in a different place in life with different awareness, these "bad beliefs" around self worth would not go away. She became angry and frustrated with herself that she could not move forward without the haunting negative beliefs that plagued her in the past. Sally wondered "What is wrong with me? Why can't I feel better about myself? Why do these beliefs keep coming up?". One day, after Sally had opened up more awareness and had a better understanding of energy, something changed. As she was questioning the thoughts of low self worth, she felt an energetic sensation in the body. Sally had noticed this sensation before but did not think to look into it. This time,

Sally was brave enough to look more into it. As she asked herself about this sensation, the self worth dragon appeared to her. At first, Sally was disgusted and repulsed. "Aha, I found the root of my lack of self worth, value, and lack of deserving, and it's you". Rather than slaying the dragon right away and casting it out of her, Sally took a different approach because she now knew so much more about the inner workings of the mind. She knew that if the dragon was within her, there must be a reason. So many questions arose in Sally's mind. "I see how strong you are. How did you come to be? What are you protecting? How have you influenced me without me noticing?".

The dragon had not been fed in a long time because Sally did not produce the same types of thoughts that had previously kept the dragon well fed. The thoughts like "I am worthless", "I don't deserve love and attention", "Stay small I will be safe", and general hateful thoughts created this dragon and kept it fed in the past. Off of these thoughts the dragon could grow and remain within this space unhindered. Now, the dragon was very hungry and weak from hiding since Sally did not produce the "food" for it anymore. It had also noticed that the former version of Sally was ready to join and integrate into the current Sally and the new belief system. Since the past version did not want to be separate anymore, the dragon would not have anything to protect. The present Sally knew how to keep herself safe without the assistance of the dragon and the negative thoughts. The dragon wanted to continue to exist. It explained to Sally what it stood for and how it had worked to protect. This showed Sally that the dragon was not "the villain", it had actually worked very hard and did a good job in the role of holding her self worth. Sally had an idea. She could change the dragon with a little effort. She could show the dragon that it was valued and appreciated rather than being neglected while explaining what new beliefs she wanted the dragon to hold. Once Sally explained to the dragon that she wanted to carry the self worth beliefs of "I am worthy, valuable, and deserving no matter what happens of what I do in life", and the dragon accepted it, the transformation was complete.

Next, Sally gathered up all of the past parts of herself that created the dragon in the first place and what it fed on. She allowed all of the parts to speak and be seen. She made sure all of these parts wanted to keep the dragon they had all become so fond of now that the dragon's vibration had shifted. They had all cared for the dragon for so long they had become attached to it and agreed to keep it. Sally and the past parts of herself started to build a house for the dragon to protect. They got to work building the stone foundation with stones infused with feelings of love, self acceptance, grace, self forgiveness, compassion, and safety. The parts reinforced the house with steel beams infused with determination, strength, and ferocity of belief. When they were finished, the parts had a camp out in it and became closer. One day soon, they would all become one.

The new foundation is what the new version of Sally is going to be made with. All of these parts would live together in harmony, safety, and of knowing Sally's true worth. Now they were no longer stuck in the past, they were in the present and future. They would be here actively feeding the dragon with thoughts of high self worth and deserving so the dragon could grow strong once again. The dragon would now protect the creation of the new version of Sally. Instead of working against her past parts and dragon, now all of them could work together over time to build the house with all of the new beliefs she chooses for herself.

Energy/Aura

Grounded Or Ungrounded Finding Middle Way Of Being

In this section, we leave the emotional/mental and enter energy concepts. This first section has to do with how we relate to our physical body. This is important for manifesting, mental clarity, psychic protection, the ability to embody our soul, increased consciousness just to name a few things.

At the start of our journey, we are often one or the other. Goal to embody the soul/higher self or whatever resonates along these lines. Regardless of which way you start the key is trust and feeling safe in the body or using our gifts. Doing inner work is thus helpful, foundation matters.

The human experience is a bit traumatic, and constricting. Some of us were not able to feel safe in our body/environment, likely causing a type of hypervigilance with the psychic senses. Those who use drugs tend to have a more expanded aura like this also. Or, were so afraid of what they sensed or people were not supportive possibly, both causing a pulling into the body and a psychic shutdown/not accepting received.

That is a basic and very general theory I have from my observations. So, with this understanding, let's go into how to approach each way and the development of abilities. Assuming this is why you are reading this. You can just work with frequencies. You do not have to work with spirit or other energies to raise your vibration. Just sit with the intent to be in higher frequencies and you will have all lower frequencies in the self come up to be removed and made aware of if need be. This way does not mean you bypass inner work/hard stuff. You may find psychic awareness just naturally increases.

While working from either angle, to be the best level of connection for the human experience, it is important to remember that all energy has information, all matter has energy. So, our body is a great way to practice psychic awareness. Our energy can be a baseline in which we compare all other vibrations/frequencies. Know thy self. Knowing your antenna also helps trust. Is it mine? Learning the connection between the body and its response to different energies is beneficial for sure. For myself, I had a reduction in anxiety just from this type of knowledge.

Ungrounded your focus should more be on learning about somatic and deep body connecting. You need to feel safe in your body, which means working on the nervous system. That's right, Fight, Flight Freeze. Your awareness of when these states are activated is going to be important. The more grounded you are, the less static you will pick up on when doing psychic work as well as moment to moment. It is healthy because to be grounded you need a calmer nervous system which is just healthy. I theorize that a lot of ADD/ADHD etc. is caused by Fight/Flight/Freeze ungrounded states. I know for myself that once I became rooted in my body, my mental clarity increased a ton. The first way I notice a lack of grounding in myself now is more random thoughts. I theorize that part of my consciousness is taken up by being aware of my body when grounded so it notices the information the subconscious is picking up less. I admit that it was not until November 2023 that I have truly experienced being grounded.

Here are some things to try.

1. Bioenergetics (a system of physical and psychological therapy that is held to increase well-being by releasing blocked physical and psychic energy. Worth the YouTube search for exercises to try).

2. Picture the root chakra spinning slower. Survival mode often causes this to move faster. It is supposed to be the slowest rotating chakra. Root chakra has to do with safety, fast spinning is not a safe feeling. I felt a definite "suck down" of energy in my body when doing this. Spirit had me do this in my preparation for trance Mediumship.

3. Be creative, mindful/slow movement, Yoga, Qi Gong/Tai Chi are all great.

Grounded your focus is going to be more on feeling energy in your body and becoming open to perception of energy outside your body. Focusing more on the space between matter, and the feeling of different vibrations in the body. Learning to listen and feel the energy within. If you find this is easy and you are more wanting to focus on developing mediumship, then you need to focus on how you receive and "looking" outside your body. Putting your awareness in the space just outside your body for about 3-6 feet to start. You want to feel your energy expand out while also feeling safe. The more you feel the energy in your own body and system the easier it is to notice the fluctuations in that system when it is interacting with the outside energies.

All these things apply to everyone. It depends a lot on where you are, these are general ideas. For psychics receiving your experience with the body is the information used as a reference. The more your 5 physical senses are experienced in a deep way the more info for the 6 th sense to use to communicate.

Empowerment Methods

Vibrations and frequencies will be used interchangeably. Psychic Protection, Attachments, and other people's energy affecting our own beginning concepts

Being grounded is a great form of psychic protection. If your soul is fully occupying your body, it's much more challenging for things to find resonance or space. It is important to claim your sovereignty and revoke permission or to just deny outside power to influence you in any way. The weaknesses with this are your own belief in your power, right to do so, and ability.We can be disempowered by the conditioning of society, family, or whatever. One of the reasons to do your inner/shadow work.

"To know yourself as the Being underneath the thinker, the stillness underneath the mental noise, the love and joy underneath the pain, is freedom, salvation, enlightenment." Eckhart Tolle[1]

Let us remember this is a journey. Many things affect our ability to feel safe or protected physically. I am not going to judge anyone's views on this. I share my views and experiences. To help with a state of empowerment from the start we will start with this example.

You know those times when you are around someone and their mood affects your mood? Good or bad on some level, you not owning your power allows the person's energy to influence your own energy. Now most of the time when a person is in a good mood it's not a problem. When someone is in a bad mood how likely are you to be influenced by that mood? If the person is not saying anything to you, this is an example of frequency resonance. A simple imagination of a bubble and observing the other person's energy doing something when it hits yours. (floating away, reflecting back, mirror, or shifting to a higher vibration). Play with it and use what will work for you. The Bubble Exercise is great for developing this.

---

1. *https://www.brainyquote.com/authors/eckhart-tolle-quotes*

When dealing with most things, thought forms, and beings with a body, the statement/affirmation "I deny your power" works wonders. Even when dealing with the topic below it will likely work just great. It has to do with your belief in your power that it will work etc. If you have problems with disempowerment, self-worth etc and find it does not work, then look into that. We are the key and have the power. Change the programs and you change your power level.

There are mediums, energy workers, and healers who choose to not be as curious as I am and do not have any problems being protected. Higher frequencies are not comfortable to lower frequencies. That is why sometimes things come up (emotions/memories/patterns etc) when we get attunements or are working to consistently raise our frequency. It is also a form of protection having a high frequency. This topic also really brings home the importance of energetic maintenance.

I however am very curious about other energy beings, usually trying some form of communication or understanding of what it is, and if there is resonance between us, try to find it within myself and heal. I don't get out much and these have been good catalysts. Instead of people triggering me, energies did.

It is very important to note here that when we claim and truly own our energy system these interferences are less, as we are conscious of the phenomena and believe in our power. There are no/less unconscious/subconscious permissions.

The point of this is that by acknowledging frequency resonance and that there may be thought forms, random energies, or beings with no body, that due to emotional wounds/trauma, etc, have resonance somewhere within us. At this point, we have the power and choice to become aware when the resonance within us is being aggravated or poked. Then to tell the thing we "see" them and heal it so it does not affect us. If you find more of some emotion and can not find an obvious reason, this can be an indication of such energies. Energy cords with humans are also possibilities. Knowing the difference is possible. I have found this to be a very useful thing on my journey.

You are an amazing powerful being. Fear is a trap when dealing with energies. It is a very low frequency causing subconscious doors/permissions. To have discernment one must realize and sometimes have experiences to gauge against to be discerning. I believe that we are all one. I do not see things as evil, good, or bad. I highly suggest reading "Law of the One", a channeled text of RA. It allows me to look at all energies I have come across from a place of love and respect. What can I learn about myself from this? Curiosity will reduce the power of fear.

If you want to work with your guides and spirit, you need to be discerning. There are fake guides. Trust your gut. Guides are not at all pushy and you can question them without anything but love as a reply. Not saying all things are good or bad either. Some are joker types or just curious thus more neutral. That said best to know for sure before taking advice or channeling (people channel frequently and don't know it)

Yes, I do call in help in the form of angels or even "whatever frequency will help me at this time". Fear gives your power away. To stand your ground and "I deny influence, claim my Sovereignty, I deny your power here, thank you for coming to visit but you will to go now" and wait till it is not perceivable anymore. Most of the time they leave quickly, their strength is subtleness, once you notice them they lose any advantage they may have had. Sometimes they may test you a little but hold your frequency and ground from a place of love and understanding. You can likely just stand in your power and say something like, you have no power here over and over until you don't notice them anymore. You are not alone even calling on your higher/true self/soul works.

This does increase the importance of knowing one's self and emotions.

For those looking to work with spirit. There are spectrums of frequency so if there are angels there then must be the opposite opposites. Trust yourself. There was a good year or so I was working with a false guide. It was not until I tried trance and had the medium I was working with confirm the distrust tugging at the back of my mind in regards to it. Not to say it was bad but it was a little pushy and had a little ego "I'm so awesome look what we can do together" type of thing.

I have always been very curious on my journey of energies and so I explored all different vibrations. Elementals, or other "make believe" things I highly suspect are real, just not in physical form. It is just a matter of perceiving these things. Take a gnome for example. Really a harmless being. A bit dense in energy but it feels neutral.

I find it very helpful to have a method to gauge the frequency of a being. I know someone who, with spirit, set up a thermometer. I use a clock. From 12-6 are humans WITH A BODY, elementals, and denser energies as the base of what they are. From 6-12 - are those that can be of the light, even if they have some stuck heavy energy, they are at the core able to be of the light. (ETs, guides, angles, soul retrieval/rescue transition etc.) Just as a quick thing, there have been some very strange experiences where this is not the case but for me, this is a way I can quickly check. Spirit will help you. These are just examples. If you are not interested in having contact and learning from other vibrational beings, you can and should set that intent. There are mediums and others who make this choice. No judgment either, we are all one and have important roles to play.

Besides heavy or light, there is also fast and slow. You can have something that is dense energy that vibrates fast. Is this an "evil" bad thing? It's definitely not an angel, though it's just as smart if a bit manipulative and is of the service to self-polarity (a reference to the law of the one), so it's best to not make any agreements or interact much with it. In my most recent interaction with one such, I noticed it had an influence on the frequency of ego needing to be a special type of wound. It was not a fun thing for me to look at within myself and get to know, but I am glad I did.

In closing of this topic, you are the one with power over your frequency. You can come up with some power statements; this is not a new concept. A search will provide some examples. Awareness also gives you power. When learning to be a medium or energy healer you learn to hold your frequency while interacting with another's frequency. Psychics do this also but are maybe not as intentional. Your intent, self-belief, and belief in the help you call in if you call someone is the key to energetic protection.

Experiencing Energy, Vibrations
Psychic Development

These exercises can help feel empowered and confident in the topic just discussed. Understand on a deeper level what we really are. Connecting us to everything in a way we can experience how we are the same. Foundation is important when developing our intuition or psychic abilities. Experiencing energy is a large part of my journey and moment to moment life.

Starting with the only limits are the ones placed/imposed by yourself, known or unknown. It is all just communication between the conscious and the subconscious. At some point you will not need these for the most part, everything will come automatically. You will have built trust in your perception ability and gifts. The real way these exercises work and the reason you want to use them is to open your conscious mind to the FACT and begin believing you're able to perceive this information.

Some of these are constructs to help with intent to do the thing or get the information. Some can be used to track over time your progress. These for the most part you can do alone. I used them all after a "level up" or big energy clearing to reset my confidence. None of it is set in stone, adapt or explore what may work best for you. These will all help with all areas including Healing, psychic, mediumship, and the sensing of the truth of what you and the world are. Vibration/Frequency. Remember it is very subtle, don't give up, and don't doubt if you think you feel something. You are feeling/perceiving it. Trust has to start somewhere, so have fun and play it creates less resistance in your system.

Auras are just energy vibrating. Cells are energy vibrating. Vibrations affect matter. Have you ever done sound healing or felt the beat in your cells with loud music? Why not try these with the intent to perceive the vibrations of the physical matter of things and then the energetic body of it? If you try on yourself first, it gives a baseline experience. Soft, hard, fast, slow, light, heavy, dense are just some basic things. Cycle through all your physical senses. If you ask yourself and are open to how you perceive these things. Who is to say vibration does not have a taste, smell, or color? Because it is just about you learning this extra sense like a child learning to talk or walk. Be kind to yourself.

In every activity here, set the intent that you WANT, CAN, AND DO perceive the info of the exercise, everyone is different and will have slightly or vastly different experiences. I will not go into seeing the aura with clairvoyance. This is about using the body as what it is, an antenna. When doing these feel free to (ethically) gain information using the chairs(non-physical receptors. Aka psychic abilities) if you wish to expand on them. You can always take very basic things and increase the difficulty by slightly shifting the intent to sense more. The observations from doing these will help give a deeper fundamental understanding through direct experience. In the long run, it will help with in-person and remote energy sensing.

Remember to Play and have fun. Try different ways of breathing and even feeling contrasting emotions, anger/love, and see what the results are. Contracting or expanding? You are learning, exploring: be kind to yourself.

Exercise One

Energy/Aura Sensing

Using your hands is one of the easiest ways to feel the physical body's energy. You know magnets when the two ends repel or push away from each other? If you get your hand chakras activated a little this repelling feeling is a way to perceive your energy.

1. To activate the chakras you can imagine an eye or opening in the center of the hands. Gently rub your hands together (not creating friction) then shake them a few times. The goal is to feel some kind of sensation or tingling may be very little in the center of your hands.

2. Starting at about shoulder-width apart. Palms facing each other move your hands slowly together.

3. Start taking deep breaths and thinking of love will always increase the energy flow and feelings.

4. Your goal here is to feel at some point before your hands touch a pushing away from each other or a stronger sensation of some kind in the hands the closer you get.

5. Over time you may feel more resistance or even heat. Depending also on mood, and physical health. Try feeling different emotions(which are vibrations) What did you notice?

I remember the first time I saw this. My friend had me put my hand between her two hands. It was HOT, the air between felt like it was burning me. Along my journey, I have noticed my feelings with this exercise change. Healing hands is a real thing.

Now this can go even further.

1. While still using your hand to sense, try it with different plants, trees, pets, or even people. You're looking for a slight resistance feeling the aura of the thing. Like pushing against a bubble but like a soap bubble, it doesn't take much to get past the barrier. This is subtle work. Imagine trying to touch a soap bubble and not pop it but feel the surface. Feeling smoke or a heat wave are also examples.

2. The larger the item the further you should start. For myself, I found when doing with a tree starting 4 feet out and slowly walking with my hands out I started to pick up something around 3 feet. With two people, start about 6-7 Feet. maybe you will even notice with your whole body. You know that sensation when someone comes up behind you.

3. Be open to any information you may get. Feelings, colors, smells. Let your imagination run. What is the tree telling you with its energy? What is its sex, or personality? Start allowing and opening to information it doesn't have to feel right. Try not to judge yourself.

Nex,t is using our hands and feeling our energy in the body. Some people refer to this or something similar as "running energy". Where you pay attention to the feeling of earth and source/god etc energy moving in the body. You just intended (people find using a color) to feel the energy as you visualize the energy coming from the ground into your feet, from above, and into you. How are these energies different? There are many videos on it. I even have one if you check my YT channel. We are going to skip right to sensing the energy centers and using our hands to move energy in the body here.

1. You can start anywhere. The main point is to feel the physical sensation in the body of the chakra or energy center. This is also the basics of Hands-on healing methods. Reiki starts at the top, other methods start at the bottom. Start where you need help. If you are grounded, start at the top. If you're ungrounded, start at the root. You can use this to balance and work with your energy system. Be sure to set an intent and focus on feelings of love and caring when doing this for the best effect, breath moves energy so go with the flow if you feel like breathing a certain way. Do not hold your breath!

2. If the hand placements are not comfortable, you can focus your attention and imagine gold/white light at the spot. It can be just as effective.

3. On your first few times hold your hand just above the spot until you feel some sort of physical sensation. You can start at your feet and place your hands on all the joints up/down including the hands and wrists.

4. When doing this, be sure to breathe and allow any emotions/energy to be released. It is not an uncommon thing to yawn, have tears with no emotion, and tingling heat/cooling.

5. You can hold your hand above the main chakra points along the spine and try to feel if they are open/closed/balanced with your hand floating just above. Experience will be important to tell the difference. Maybe you have had someone do this type of scan if you had reiki.

With the mention of Reiki let's get into the basics of Healing. I found the methods above helped me to link the effects of thought and emotion on my chakras. It brings a deeper layer of truth to the statement we are energy.

Healing Basics

The first thing to note is that the healer is the holder of the frequency and does not do the actual healing. The person who receives it does it. It is their system (energy/body) that goes to match the frequency/vibration of the healer. Even the belief that the person receiving the healing plays a role. The more belief the client has the higher success. The energy will go where it needs to go regardless of where the hands are.

- These are the basics of healing modalities. Some healers channel other energies (mediumship or Reiki for example), and some use just their own. In the occult/esoteric it is referred to as Auric Magnetism/Magnetic Healing

- The higher the vibration the better it works. Thinking of something you love while doing it produces good results.

Placing hands on an injury does help and work. If you have done the above exercises and played with breath and feelings you likely noticed a difference in the hand sensations. Healing is effective in person and at a distance. Energy knows no time or space.

Working With The Aura

Next, I would recommend what I refer to as "energetic space awareness". Here you will start to focus on the energy outside your body. This is to open the mind to the possibility and a construct for sensing where things are located in your aura. As well as to introduce the concept that you can tap in specifically to any layer of the aura and where that is from your body. Why would you want to know this? I have found it helpful with my mediumship, feeling connected and one with everything, and was also empowered regarding my energy knowledge of self. This all comes to increasing awareness of self and another layer of consciousness. There are many paths to oneness, connectedness, leveling up, enlightenment, or whatever your goal is. This is the way I have searched for it. I did not know until I started some of these exercises and experiences that it was the knowledge I was seeking.

This has an empowering effect as well as it also allows you to link the experience between physical sensations and the expansion/contraction of the aura. I have found the more experience I have with feeling energies the more connected I feel to the creator.

The Bubble Exercise

The basic idea here is that when you breathe IN you intend to sense your aura contracting. When you breathe OUT you intend to feel your aura expand. Maybe you have sensed something similar before. You can try just doing in and out or you can do the full exercise. For the best experience of doing this, you will want to get your energy flowing and fueled by earth and source. See basic recharge/cleansing for this if you do not have a method. Pay attention to how your body feels before and after all parts of this and during if you can. Feel the difference in the body with the intent of energy density.

Doing this can sometimes feel a little scary if you are used to your energy being overly grounded or expanded. There may be a little anxiety so stop as soon as you start to feel uncomfortable. Look into that, and ask yourself: why? Often our energy state is due to some survival need. As For myself, I was overextended/hyper-vigilant. The key is do not push this should be a fun exploratory empowering method/tool for energy control.

Some ways to visualize this are thick(in/condensed) or thin(expanded) smoke, balloon or soap bubbles, or even saran wrap. To help with the concept of expanded or contracted and visualizations.
Grounded

1. If you are generally a GROUNDED person you will want to expand first because you are naturally more condensed energetically. For other tips see the other chapters.

2. With every IN breath, you will fill up more source/earth energy

3. When you *EXHALE/OUT* imagine your energy pushing *OUT* just a little.

4. The next breath more is flowing into you so when you breathe out there is plenty of energy.

5. You should be breathing slowly with strong intent that your energy does not come in when you inhale.

6. When you notice a difference in the body or feel expanded, set the intent that in the next set of breaths, your aura will settle into a perfectly healthy protected state

7. Now inhale and exhale. What does your energy do? Did it come in as far as before? How does this feel in your body?

Ungrounded

1. If you are generally UNGROUNDED you are going to want to start by contracting aura.

2. On every breath IN you're going to imagine your energy coming *IN* just a little each time.

3. Slowly EXHALE with the strong intent your energy does not go out.

4. Pay attention to your body. It may start to not be a comfortable feeling (does it remind you of when you are afraid? The energy comes inward/more dense as protective in fear. Fear makes the aura contract. Here we are doing that without fear.

5. Set the intent on the next set of breaths for your aura to go to a healthy protective state. How does this feel? Did your energy go out as far? Do you feel more grounded?

You can bounce your aura by having it go in and out with each breath for fun or the intent to get it to a healthy (not too open not too closed) state or after maybe doing a full body shaking bioenergetics. I still use this exercise to clear my energy or just connect and self-check.

Again you can take this further. Usually, I introduce this when doing mediumship. However, it is easily adapted. The goal here is to increase awareness of where things are in your aura. This can build off of the other basics when you sense things with your hands. This just allows for stretching your awareness.

You can do this anywhere. Sensing anything as it's on the outer edge of the aura and closer to the body. Some examples I have played with

- When walking, sense the vegetation as you pass it. As it moves into and through your aura.

- As a passenger in a car sensing the people in the car next to you pass through your energy. The same goes for walking around people.

- When sitting try to feel the auras and energy of the bugs and small animals around without using your hands. This is remote viewing/sensing.

- In mediumship, we would invite the spirit to go in and out. Further and closer and perceive where in our energy space they are.

Notice how your body feels as things are close or far in your energetic space. I found tingling gets more or less intense. All of this is bringing things naturally observed on a subconscious level into consciousness. It is possible and more with practice. This helps to understand the link between mental/emotional impacts on the body. How the body stores energy. To feel the energy allows us to add extra intent with our deeper understanding, building belief results in better healing results.

Energetic Responsibility Mechanics
Energy Clearing

Great now with a better understanding through actual experience via feeling of energy time to get serious. If you are empathic, this may be very helpful.

As you become aware of yourself in this way you can become more responsible and empowered. Cleaning your energy has more depth because you are even more in tune, or whatever word you want to use. When you are done talking, texting, or being on the internet, intentionally call your energy back to yourself. When we talk to people on the phone, for example, we automatically make an energy connection. It is how you feel your friend's feelings over the phone. Set the intention to notice when you have not called your energy back, maybe have a connection that is still open. Over time you will be able to tell. Maybe you have heard of cord-cutting. Well, why not be able to sense the cords of all of them you have? All you need is an open mind, intent and practice. These concepts are helpful.

- Every time you interact with someone imagine a sticky hand. You know those you could get from a machine? Or even a fishing line with a sensor of some kind at the end. This goes out to connect with the energy of the person you're talking to. If you know how the other person on the line is feeling. Think of this as a visual "how to" of getting information. Now you can decide how much information you want. How big is the cord opening? How sensitive is the hand or sensor at the other end? It's your choice what you would like to become aware of.

- At the end either make the opening smaller (I find with close friends a hair-type cord tends to stay connected) or disconnect. If you find this is a struggle there may be a subconscious reason, look into cord-cutting somewhere.

- If you think of the person and you had disconnected you may find you need to again or they were thinking of you and in doing so unknowingly sent a little line to you.

Know when someone is going to call? Remember, this is already happening. This is a construct you can use, to add intent and control your energy.

Now you have a construct to control your energy. And now you're gaining sensitivity or more of an idea of what was going on. With energy work confidence matters. Another construct for psychic protection in regards to cords with people. ArchAngel Michael is known to help with this if you feel the need for a hand.

- Use a glass wall/bubble with no-stick oil on it. Just slides right off with a message "Return to sender with love not welcome here" "denied entry" etc the key is to come from a place of love and belief. Sometimes there is a subconscious reason, often some disempowering belief or connection if this does not work. Going within and healing it usually fixes it. At least in my experience. We can talk to the higher self of people this way as well. "I can not help you" "Please go online to book" etc can be communicated. This is all just my own experience. These can all be applied to energy vampires and the like as well. You may find you're able to perceive them much more easily.

● Having your energy system so that everything that hits it dissolves into love with no power or influence other than love is simple and powerful

Clearing

When on the topic of energy this is both popular and important. We unknowingly make subconscious agreements causing attachments or creations as thought forms. My intent is not to cause fear here. Knowledge is power. Just as there are frequencies on all spectrums so are the attachment possibilities. They are in existence just like you made from the creator. Catalysts for growth towards realizing our power and oneness.

These are all very subtle, you may see how working with the exercises above increases awareness and can be helpful. Because they are subtle they lose tons of power when we notice them and start things to remove them. Doing inner work and healing can remove what they are attached to, give them less food, less to influence and attach to. Being in your power is the best defense unfortunately for many this state is not their regular state of being. Higher frequencies are not comfortable, think of yourself like a habitat. Lower vibrations need the right habitat. Prevention is great. One of the most powerful things to do a couple times a day is something like this:

"I claim my sovereignty fully and completely. I revoke/deny any conscious or subconscious agreements and attachments from past present and future. I claim my truth that I am a being of love. I claim my power fully, completely, in every way."

One of the reasons we want to embody our soul is that our soul being in our body leaves no/less space for attachments. It is important to find the difference between what is your self/inner child other wound and something else. We do not want to be claiming something not us as us or rejecting something that is us. Energy resonance. What is the attachment in us resonating with? Work on healing that.

Attachment can be anything from a lingering energy to a full conscious entity. They can attach in childhood or day-to-day living. Think of all the in-body animals, bugs, etc in physical form. There are just as many or more co-existing in the unseen. We notice them when we raise our vibration and they are not able to camouflage anymore. Or we are trying to change habits and heal our body, mind, or spirit. They can influence and impact us on all levels. There are even soul attachments. They can feed on our emotions so look for ways to get food via triggers etc. I will share a couple of my own experiences later.

Thought forms are energy created from thoughts mixed with emotion. They often are sent out into the astral spaces but can become stuck in our own energy system. The story of the self worth dragon is an example of this. Consistent thoughts with emotion. There are books free in the references section if you want to know more. They are usually easy to clean and a reason for energetic hygiene.

Methods for general clearing there are so many ideas and constructs for this. The key to keep in mind is that your confidence level, faith, and beliefs are the main reasons any method would work. Use any of the elements and feel free to call in for help. Vibration/frequency matters. Praying is effective. Explore and experiment. You can use tools to help with intent and beliefs. However, I will stress to keep in mind that they are tools, and suggest you intend them to be temporary. Imagining rain falling or fire burning is common. For a deep scrub and extra intent have the clearing go deep into the body and cells. Feel the vibration shift even on this deeper level. Imagination is a powerful tool.

Two of my favorites are

- Standing in a huge fire that affects my energy for miles out. It also has wind that blows away the ash

- Calming water coming from the ground up through dissolving and healing pouring up over the head back down touching all the aura

- When cleaning your house you can put the intent that energy is also being cleaned in your space. Listening to happy music and being in a good vibe is needed for it to be effective. Things like sage can help as a tool. I find with house clearing you are already cleaning, allow your regular tools to be all you need. If you intend it to be so it is so. You are that powerful.

There have been many methods over the years and some I go back to. Be playful and remember your powerful, love & light.

Mediumship

First I want to touch on the types of ways we work with spirit. They are searchable terms if you desire more info.

- Healing there are many modalities this falls under. Reiki is just one, any modality where the healer's energy blended/channeled another energy has the possibility of it being spirit.

- Mental mediumship which takes place in the mind basically. Channeling messages and evidential mediumship are good examples. Rescue and transition or working with earthbound spirits are also this form of mediumship.

- Physical Mediumship basically happens outside the medium. Paranormal activity is usually this type of mediumship. Tapping, things turning on/off, opening/closing table tipping, or spirit moving things.

I am going to go with the basics here. The above exercises help your confidence, an important aspect. It is about frequency. When trying to connect, be sure to set the intent why, what/who you're connecting to, and ensure your energy is a high vibration. This is the most important thing especially when connecting alone. Use any methods to get it that way. Or example:

- Think of something you love, a person a thing etc

- Listen to music High energy music/music you like

- Dance

- Sit with the intent to have your aura infused with a high vibration and Feel it is so.

A helpful analogy here to understand the importance of your own starting vibration. It will also help with discernment. Imagine your energy as smoke of a certain thickness. It will blend and meld easily with smoke of the same thickness. When your smoke comes in contact with a smoke that is more dense it will not feel very good, on some level. As you're supposed to be at a vibration of love or joy when wanting to connect the more dense energy could be something like a sad emotion based being. You do not want to be talking or blending with this. However, a spirit that has love, joy, compassion will blend easily and smoothly with yours. You may even feel it raise your vibration.

(by doing inner work it is more comfortable and pleasant to be in the love joy in general to stay there as well as get there thus making mediumship easier in general)

Legit anything you will be much more likely to meet with beings that are that or higher vibration. Remember all of the Clair senses are applicable here. I'm not going into them with lots of info online already present. Let go of expectations of what connecting to them will be like. Intent!!!!! Doing a visualization of going up is helpful as well. Through a door then along a path to a place.

In the old days, at the start, they used to do a lot of praying and singing before connecting when in mediumship practice circles. They had no idea really who or what they were connecting with but this helped them connect with beings of love more often than not.

If you suspect already that you are connecting to spirit then pay attention to when that is. You're allowed to have any boundaries you need for where you are.

Reasons you may find boundaries are not working as yourself. Is there fear or curiosity? For myself, being hyper vigilant was an issue. My first lesson was learning that I was open or connecting all of the time and just becoming aware of this and what it felt like helped the anxiety decrease and improve empowerment.

Think about how and what role connecting with spirit will have in your life. When I first wanted to do trance many people asked me WHY? The reason matters!

It all comes down to our relationship with ourselves. The more love and acceptance we have within us on a deep level the easier a connection with spirit becomes. The more we know our energy, the faster we notice external energies.

My Journey

In this section of the book I will share more details about my journey for those interested. I will admit I had to rewrite this portion a few times. I want to be honest and to the point. I am sure many can relate to parts of my journey. Sorry if it seems ego is present I will do my best to keep the ego out of it.

Memory is strange is it not? I want to reassure you that you can do tons of healing and not have memories or remember everything. I have not gone to hypnotherapy or similar modalities. Trauma can cause amnesia. You can access what is needed by going in through the body or just tapping into the energy of emotion/thought of a time, place, or subject. Parts or aspects hold a particular theme. At least that has been my experience. I mention this because I have trauma-related amnesia and do not have many memories of under the age of ten if any. When we are ready the things we stored in the subconscious will come out in a way that we can work through, shift etc. grow or heal. I am always amazed at how what was hidden reveals itself.

The one thing I swore was a memory was in fact an inner child aspect of myself in a place I had put her. I discovered her during the year or so of counseling I did in 2017. My mom always said we were never in this place with this bed. That was the behavior I never did. I will share the experience of discovering her. I named her Rose.

My counselor had me explain the place to him first. It was a white room with a cheap white tile floor. It had a single bed with a black iron frame. With a closet. The memory that was not a memory was of me being very upset and ripping paper. I had ripped up into small pieces so much paper it was inches on the floor. It was as if small pieces of paper had snowed on the floor. I removed the door to the room many times while doing sitting work with myself that week. I felt the feelings this part held for many weeks. I talked and developed a relationship with this part. I made her a new room and visited her. I eventually learned how she influenced things in my life. I fell in love with this form of self-actualization.

That is how I began the construct of developing a relationship with myself and self-parenting. I used many of the methods mentioned in this book to meet parts of my subconscious to shift habits and patterns. At first, it mostly had to do with why I hated myself and fell back into unhealthy habits/behaviors. It is interesting to see what your subconscious allows to come up to be worked with as you develop a relationship with yourself. My journey did not start there though in 2017. That was just the time that real progress started to be made. When I started separating myself from the trauma-related programs. Prior to that, I had varying degrees of depression, a drinking problem though functional, and smoked cigarettes and pot. Comparatively, mild eating disorder and body image relationship. This is a common societal theme with the relationship between food and our bodies still I am moving along in this area as well.

I really started the self-inquiry and more spiritual journey in 2014. Nothing major, I got some free counseling at first for questions like "Why am I doing this? What am I needing, I don't want to ruin the life I have." Maybe you had a similar start to your Journey wanting to understand yourself more. I studied for a bit with some Mormons. I was raised catholic. I had a friend who was wiccan and looked into that. Tarot cards and stones/crystals, meditating or just sitting with myself, and experiencing energy. I was not consistent though. Depression and avoiding behaviors came in waves as they do. I never wanted to take medication so I floundered through it. I am always amazed that my husband stayed with me during the dark times. We were married in 2006 and had our daughter in 2008. Being a mom was the first major desire for change in myself and my programs/upbringing. "Just let her cry it out" etc., wanting to be better for her.

I did spend my time in dark depression as many of us do. My story is not so unique or different than many going through the human experience. Trauma, it seems, is the name of the game here. I never gave up wanting to love and understand myself. At some point when in the darkness of depression I surrendered and learned to find it beautiful, the pain. One turning point was when I heard someone say, something like "we are comfortable in X state, it is scary to leave". It helped me realize just what that mental state was doing. I learned to really love that vibrational state. Can you guess what I found to happen? It became impossible to get as low as my lowest low. When you're in the state and it's comforting, safe and you can love yourself when there it becomes like sand. There are so many metaphors to use: Cleaning a cup, emptying rocks, leaving luggage. This love I feel for my own lower vibrational emotions makes it much easier to interact from a place of love with other vibrational beings who deal in those vibrations. To hold space for people as they face them.

I get ridiculously excited when people are processing and transmuting their self-hate, shame, guilt, fear etc. mainly because what is on the other side is also beautiful. But I could talk about it all day. This is the reason though I focus more on the inner work than psychic and mediumship development in general. However, I know I would not be where I am without the support of spirit.

So, how does mediumship or working with Spirit have to do with this sharing of mental/emotional healing? I must say that if I did not have spirit to show me what unconditional love felt like I would not have been able to apply that to myself. I was not able to have it for anyone in my life. When I first started working with spirit just sitting with them and allowing (and thinking maybe I deserve to have) the feelings of love, compassion, and acceptance caused a strange type of emotional pain. It can be so hard to accept into yourself, we all deserve to be loved unconditionally. Spirit can do so while we learn how.

I had a space (mental construct of a clearing) when doing my sitting work where I would meet with spirit. Just to sit with them. I would just sit in their love and cry. Really, I think I just did this for a couple of months. I would allow myself to feel the feelings I had while feeling the love of spirit. Being cradled in that energy gave me the courage to just feel what feelings were there that day. I was an emotional stuffer and outside of counseling, I didn't know how to feel. As my heavy emotions poured out they replaced it with love. That is how I got through learning to feel my emotions and starting to let go of self-hate. When you're not capable of loving yourself even a little other than wanting to love yourself more, spirit is priceless. It has always been an honor to work with them. I think they helped me stay out of the places I could easily have gone. I mean as a teen a part of me wanted to be a stripper and prostitute (I learned on my journey these were past life influences). Somehow, the opportunities did not present themselves in a way that was easily manifested. My mom did help a lot too. Anyway, likely a group effort as many things likely are.

I first experienced spirit the same night I learned about mediumship. My friend Lindsay and I went to a seance in October 2017. The medium did a form of physical mediumship. She had us put two fingers lightly on a disk. The disk moved in a circle for yes and stopped for no. It was very interesting in that I could tell none of us were directing it in such a perfect circle. There was a group of 10 people including us; we went three at a time with the medium. When it came to be my turn the medium asked

Are you a female: *yes*

Are you here for (someone's name): *no*

Are you here for Wendy? : *Yes*

A question or two after that I had a connection with our family friend Heather. She had passed a few years prior. It was like she was right there, I felt the full force of her personality, I didn't see her so much as sense her there. The medium guided me by asking the questions which I got the answer from Heather. It turned out she had a message for my sister who she was much closer to when alive! Unfortunately, I do not remember the medium's name. She deserves credit for being such a beautiful helper of spirit. She pointed me in the direction of a local spiritualist church.

In 2018 I joined a closed circle with the spiritualist church for 12 weeks. This experience was very important. A safe space is essential to being able to gain the confidence to explore. Confirmation of what one is receiving and providing guidance speed things up. Watching others work with spirit and ET's as well as doing some myself was amazing and I encourage anyone to find a safe place. At this time I was doing daily sitting work at home as well as the weekly closed circle, weekly open circle, and zen practice. Basically, my evenings were dedicated to knowing myself, my energy, and spirit. I was going to counseling as well, it's amazing how it all was developed together.

I also joined Zen Head Community, where they cultivated both psychological and spiritual growth side by side. Courses with both. In 2019 I started a practice circle with other members of that group. Most of my development was with other beginners playing and exploring. We did all manner of psychic and mediumship, the time of discovery. In 2021, I took the certification for evidential mediumship through Zen. The spirit was always there. I often felt at that time unqualified for hosting a mediumship circle. Spirit gave clear messages that I should keep doing so. I continued to attend the Spiritualist church open circles until I moved in the spring of 2019.

It is hard to know what experiences to share. I suppose I will share my first non-human expense on my own. It was a shapeshifter and its lesson was about boundaries. I was questioning my ability to host more mediumship-orientated circles. We focused mostly on psychic work at that point. I was at home doing my sitting work and upon noticing an energy started just seeing how I perceived it. I could see internal clairvoyance, I could sense the "personality" of it. It was also curious. I kept getting confused though. One minute I would confirm yes it's an older woman etc., the next it was an elephant. Now the next day I asked a friend to have a "look". They were also new. My boundaries with spirit at this point were very shaky mainly because I did not have many in life in general. Adding in being curious did not help either. As well as I was working on "open" and 'closed'. It was not anything for me to have a link with something all day. I did not know too much difference still. Anyway, my friend also had this shift to a couple of different things when connecting but we didn't feel it was harmful. I did end up reaching out to the medium I sat in a closed circle with. I went to her house and she assisted me in more in-depth communication with it and she drew me a picture. I then set a boundary and it went away. The message was I needed especially in circle settings set clear boundaries and intentions. There were some times when connecting with this being that I was afraid. I as a result looked within myself. Lesson in boundaries and discernment.

Next, I will share early energy healing experiences with spirit. My first experience was receiving some "hands on healing" I think it was called. Some Sundays the Spiritual Center offered "by donation" healings after services. I stayed and got work done. They channeled spirit and did not actually touch my body at all but hovered just above it. I noticed after this that my energy through my chakras moved more easily and the information from spirit came more clearly. At this point, I was often just observing my own energy in my sitting work at home. Spirit would have me move my hands on my chakras. Just simple things observing energy in my system when alone and when spirit was blending with me. I can not remember the first time I did energy healing blended with spirit on another person. My best guess is we played during a practice circle. I find it very easy. We don't do more than blend with spirit and listen for if they needed me to move a hand somewhere or say something.

I did go for a reiki session a few times over the years or had friends do it on me. I have always been focused on the subtle differences in frequency of the energies. Experiencing the difference between Reiki energy and when working with spirit was fun. It is more work in some ways but we can attune ourselves to other frequencies like reiki. It is just easier when we have help. Just as healing with energy, we can do it ourselves but having someone hold the healing frequency allows the shifts we need to make as the one receiving to happen faster.

Just as every living human has their own frequency, so do other beings not in a body. More earth-based beings are often mentioned in fairy tales, myths, etc. These ideas come from places in the energy realms. Just not always perceivable to many. The artists of all kinds, shamans, etc who speak of the existence of these things. It is just a matter of being open to the perception. I will not mention much about this though, other than I have been curious and aware of them from early in my journey. In a circle space doing house clearings, we got confirmation from each other all perceiving a similar thing. To meet them with curiosity and love first. Just as there are bugs and plants in our physical space there are in the nonphysical. I have learned from these beings mainly about boundaries and them pointing out within myself the same frequency so I may work on it in myself. I don't spend a ton of time with them.

One of the main reasons I had a decrease in anxiety as I went along my journey was this realization. Becoming aware that I was sensing something and did not know what it was, becoming curious, and finding out helped.

My favorite thing to do with spirit is energy channeling for healing. Mainly because there is less pressure. You can set intent, observe what spirit is doing, and trust that miracles can happen. I did play with hands-on healing using the breath and just my vibrational state. It takes focus though as reiki also. A trance state is less focus. In 2022 I got Reiki Level two. I am not sure I will get my master's, I trust the opportunity will come if it is meant to be. I can see how it is good empowerment for people to do energy work. Or those who do not have a background working with spirit. In spring of 2024, I played with "high-frequency exposure" where I just sat for 20-30 min in as high of frequencies as I could. That also caused the release of limiting beliefs and programs.

The last experience I will share seems an unlikely way for spirit to help with. That is feeling grounded. In the fall of 2023, I set the intent to open my heart more. Shortly after that, I got the nudge to develop a deep trance mediumship. I had seen a friend do an amazing job of it a few years prior. They had no recollection of what spirit and those of us in the circle said to each other. I knew when setting the intent of doing this that it would require the next level of trust. Both with my relationship with spirit and myself. I have not invested much in my development at this point other than time and effort. The 12-week course was all till this point. I booked three sessions with my friend to assist with this part of my development.

In the first session, my friend spirit basically said I needed to be more grounded. That seemed silly to me. Why did I need to be in my body even more? Though really I was not really in my body much. In the weeks between my 1 and 2 sessions spirit in its way had information come to me that would help with this. If you have ever asked spirit for help with anything you know how it comes. Someone mentions something and a strong "I need to look into that". I had to look into bioenergetic exercises of which I find shaking the whole body very effective. There was some inner work I did as well. Facing some fears as I learned how to feel safe enough in my body to get into it more deeply. Long story short, in the last session I blended deeply and fully with an ET. I discovered in this period of time from about December 2023 to February 2024 a false guide I had been working with. I never fully trusted them as they had a bit more ego then I think a true guide should have. Not to say they meant harm when I worked with them but I was not willing to let go of consciousness to the extent I originally wanted to. The energy of the ET was fast, light, and just an amazing experience. It was as though I was wearing a robot suit. I definitely need more practice but I got distracted. I had learned what I needed to do for that part of the journey. A deeper trust in myself, my discernment and spirit. Though really wanting to work with spirit this way gave me that push I apparently needed to connect more with my body. To feel safe in it and keep choosing to get in it when I get out of it.

Another thing that distracted me after the third session was re-learning how to trust and receive psychic/spirit information when actually in my body. At this point, I became like a newly developing medium. However, it was not the first time something similar happened. I often took breaks from my development to do inner work. Whenever I went back to developing after such a break there was a "okay, what is new this time?" It has been my observation that the more inner work I do the more clear my readings and perception of energy is. The fact of the matter is I have likely done more Inner work then practice with spirit. The real truth is though, I get to know my own spirit and energy more in the end its the same thing. Us in a body are the same as spirit so all the work translates. If we are afraid of something within us when we perceive that outside ourselves we will be afraid. We are all the same. The information all comes from the same place in the end. Source god etc. I feel I have fallen in love with the human experience and do not claim to know any or all answers. I just keep looking and asking for help. Developing my relationship with myself, source spirit and whatever comes along. One day I will leave my body until then I will do what I am here to do. Learn and experience. The business aspect of my Journey really is just to continue to learn. Yes, I want to be of service to others and help. But a part of helping do that is continuing to heal and know myself.

Well, I think that sums up my journey part of this book. I am learning just like you are. Feel free to reach out by email, or comments on socials if you want to know more about something. I would love to hear how this book impacted you. Happy to make content using your questions. In the next section, I share references but encourage you to ask Spirit for guidance and to bring in information. It is your journey trust yourself. What resonates today may not resonate tomorrow. An example of this in my Journey is the Paul Seilg Books. I heard of them a few times earlier in my journey from one person or another. It was not until 2023 that I got the "I need to see what this is about" nudge. You are at the perfect place in your journey at all times there is no right or wrong, ahead or behind. I hope you go forward with curiosity, forgiveness, and love for yourself thus everything around you. With anything take what resonates and leave the rest, no one has all the truth/answers. Only ever a part, don't you think? Where would be the mystery and questing otherwise?

References and Terms

Internal Family Systems

(IFS) is a form of psychotherapy developed by Dr. Richard C. Schwartz in the 1980s. It is based on the idea that the mind is made up of multiple sub-personalities or "parts," each with its own unique perspectives, feelings, and memories. IFS assumes that these parts can become disordered but can be healed through a process of self-exploration and self-compassion.

Memory reconciliation

is a process used in psychotherapy to help individuals integrate and resolve traumatic or distressing memories. The goal is to reduce the emotional impact of these memories and alter their influence on the person's current behavior and emotional state. Various therapeutic approaches utilize memory reconciliation, including Eye Movement Desensitization and Reprocessing (EMDR), Internal Family Systems (IFS), and other trauma-focused therapies.

Books and Authors

- Healing the Fragmented Selves Of Trauma Survivors by Janina Fisher

- Dark side of the Light Chasers Debbie Ford

- Psychic Self Defense and other books by Dion Fortune

- The Human Aura Astral colours and Thought Forms + Genuine Medium or The Invisible Powers By William walker Atkinson (public Domain Book)

- Thought Forms By Charls Webster Leadbeater (public Domain Book)

- Cosmic consciousness and healing with the quantum Field by Darshan Baba

- Emotion or Body Code by Dr. Bradly Nelson

- Quantum Touch By Richard Gordon

- Mastering Mediumship Albert Olson

- I am Word series by Paul Selig

- Joe Dispenza Breaking the Habit of being yourself

- Matrix reimprinting with EFT tapping

- The body keeps the score by Bessel van der Kolk

- Waking the tiger by Peter Levine

- Whatever Arises by Matt Khan

Topics

The law of the one channeled text of Ra is easy to Google. I enjoyed the study guide

Anything Quantum Mechanics

Somatic exercises/experiencing and Bioenergetics

Veil of reality bernhard guenther has good psycho-spiritual information

YouTube I will not put too much here as part of your journey will be finding people who resonate best with you per topic

- Zen Rose Garden/David A. Caren - has Great self love, psychic and mediumship information. I am still part of their FB group. They had a lot to do with the beginning of my journey.

- Aaron Abke condenses some of the RA and other spiritual teachings in an easy to understand and apply way.

- Irene Lyon-great somatic understanding and practice information

- Astral Door Way

About the Author

Wendy is a wife and mom, certified medium, level two reiki practitioner, intuitive healer, and coach/mentor with a passion for inner child work. She talks about self-growth methods, psychic/mediumship, and other topics she learned in the ten years of her own growth.

Read more at https://linktr.ee/wendos_light.